M000019671

the little book of
RESILIENCE

lucy lane

summersdale

THE LITTLE BOOK OF RESILIENCE

Copyright © Summersdale Publishers Ltd, 2016

With research by Katherine Bassford

An Hachette UK Company
www.hachette.co.uk

Summersdale Publishers Ltd
Part of Octopus Publishing Group Limited
Carmelite House
50 Victoria Embankment
LONDON
EC4Y 0DZ
UK

www.summersdale.com

Printed and bound in the Czech Republic

ISBN: 978-1-84953-830-5

Substantial discounts on bulk quantities of Summersdale books are available to corporations, professional associations and other organisations. For details contact general enquiries: telephone: +44 (0) 1243 771107 or email: enquiries@summersdale.com

INTRODUCTION

Life has its ups and downs, and knowing how to adapt to adversity is essential to our health and happiness. Resilience is the ability to bounce back from the difficulties we all face. The good news is that psychologists have identified methods and strategies that enable us to navigate through crisis and overcome misfortune. This little book is packed with encouraging quotations and simple tips to help you build your inner strength and weather the tough times with hope and resolve.

LOOK FOR THE SILVER LINING

Mentally strong people have the ability to see the positives in tough circumstances. Rather than seeing the world through rose-coloured glasses, they recognise that it's possible for good things to come from hardship. This doesn't erase the hardship, but it can make it easier to cope with. The next time you face a challenge, ask yourself, 'What can I learn from this? What is this an opportunity for? How can this positively affect me?'

If you're going through hell, keep going.

Winston Churchill

MAKE IT A HABIT

Mental toughness or 'grit' can be cultivated. Think of it as a muscle which needs to be worked in order to grow stronger. To exercise your 'grit muscle', push yourself in small ways on a daily basis. Resist the snooze button in the morning and get up and go for a run. Turn off the TV and write a paragraph of the book you've been saying for ages you want to write. Move the trickiest task to the top of your to-do list at work. By practising mental toughness in tiny ways, you will prove to yourself over and over that you have what it takes. Mentally tough people are not more intelligent or talented than the average person; they're more consistent. Practise 'grit' on a regular basis. Good things happen at the edge of your comfort zone.

When you come
to a **roadblock**,
take a detour.

Mary Kay Ash

However long the night,
the dawn will break.

African proverb

FOCUS ON YOUR STRENGTHS

Many people base their sense of self-worth on external factors such as what others think of them or what job they do. As a result, their confidence is extremely unstable – an 'off' remark or a bad day at work can cause their self-esteem to plummet. The key to resilience is to base your sense of self-worth on who you authentically are. One way of doing this is to identify and focus on your unique strengths. Think of a time when you did something you were really proud of. Now think about the strengths, skills and talents you used to make this happen. Were you creative, organised, determined, brave or thoughtful? Repeat this process with several other positive events and look to see which strengths make regular appearances. These are your signature strengths. Know that you carry these with you wherever you go. You can deploy these strengths whenever you're faced with a challenge, such as moving home, starting a new relationship or changing career. Embracing your strengths will give you confidence in your ability to handle any challenge that comes your way.

There was never a night
or a problem that could
defeat sunrise or hope.

Bernard Williams

CHOOSE YOUR RESPONSE

We all experience bad days and crises in our lives, but how we respond to these situations is up to us. When something 'bad' happens, we can choose to react negatively, or we can opt to remain calm and look for a solution. Often our reactions are habits we've fallen into. It's important to realise you always have a choice. When faced with a setback, pause for a moment and consciously decide how you would like to respond.

FIND YOUR CALLING

A sense of purpose can enable us to overcome challenges which might otherwise overwhelm us. It can give us the determination to keep going, despite discomfort. This is best summed up by a quote from the philosopher Nietzsche: 'He who has a why to live can bear almost any how.' To find your purpose, identify what you're drawn to. Which moments make you feel authentic, as if you are doing something you were truly made for? Perhaps you have experienced this feeling when organising a charity event, nursing a sick animal, or creating a work of art. You may have also experienced 'flow', which is a state in which you're so immersed in what you're doing that time seems to disappear. Look at what gives your life meaning and trust what your heart tells you. A strong sense of purpose will fill you with motivation and enthusiasm, and help you to transcend the ups and downs of life.

DO NOT BE EMBARRASSED BY YOUR FAILURES. LEARN FROM THEM AND START AGAIN.

Richard Branson

The bamboo that bends is stronger than the oak that resists.

Japanese proverb

IF AT FIRST YOU DON'T SUCCEED...

It is continuous effort – not talent or intelligence – that holds the key to success in life. Successful people understand this. As a result, they are action-oriented. Of course, sometimes it makes sense to quit, but don't make the mistake of giving up too early. Walt Disney's first animation company went bankrupt and he was reputedly turned down 302 times before he got financing for creating Disneyland. Equally, J. K. Rowling was living on the breadline before she found success with Harry Potter, but only after 12 publishers rejected her manuscript. Ask yourself, are you looking for a quick fix? Do you have a tendency to give up when things get tough? Or do you persevere and keep trying to find a way to make things work? Commit to keep going until you reach your goal.

If you learn from defeat,
you haven't really lost.

Zig Ziglar

THIS TOO SHALL PASS

When you're going through a tough time, it can feel as if things will never change. Perhaps you move to a new location, struggle to make friends, and think you will always be alone. Or your relationship ends and you feel as if the pain and heartache will never stop. Whatever the situation, remind yourself that 'this too shall pass'. What is stressful now will be just a memory within a few weeks, months or years. Nothing lasts forever. Everything changes with time, especially the way you see things.

While we may lose **heart**, we never have to lose **hope**.

H. Jackson Brown Jr

To persevere is important for everybody. Don't give up, don't give in. There's always an answer to everything.

Louis Zamperini

HELP SOMEONE ELSE

Volunteering can be a great way to distance yourself from your troubles. It will shift your focus from yourself to others and can help you put things into perspective. You could volunteer regularly at a food bank, or simply look for opportunities to help a neighbour, friend or colleague. Studies show that volunteering reduces depression, increases happiness and self-esteem, and boosts our sense of being in control of our lives.

People often say that motivation doesn't last. Well, neither does bathing – that's why we recommend it daily.

Zig Ziglar

WHAT'S YOUR EXPLANATION?

The way you explain life's setbacks to yourself is important. Psychologists say that an optimistic (and therefore more resilient) 'explanatory style' is composed of three main elements. Firstly, optimistic people view the effects of bad events as being temporary rather than permanent. For example, instead of saying 'My boss never thanks me for my hard work', they might say 'My boss didn't thank me for the work I did on that project'. Secondly, resilient people don't let setbacks affect unrelated areas of their life. For instance, they would say 'I'm not very good at cooking' rather than 'I'm no good at anything'. Finally, resilient people don't blame themselves when bad events occur. They see other people or circumstances as being the cause. So, if they get made redundant, they're likely to say 'The company doesn't have much work at the moment' rather than 'I was lousy at my job!' People with an optimistic explanatory style tend to be happier, healthier and more successful at work, school and in sport. Those with a pessimistic explanatory style are more prone to depression, anxiety and low self-esteem.

WHEN YOU HAVE EXHAUSTED ALL POSSIBILITIES, REMEMBER THIS: YOU HAVEN'T.

Thomas Edison

Scar tissue is stronger
than regular tissue.
Realise the strength,
move on.

Henry Rollins

PRACTISE GRATITUDE

Taking time to acknowledge what is good in your life can make all the difference when adversity strikes. Studies show that gratitude lifts our spirits and floods our body with feel-good hormones. How you practise gratitude is up to you. You could end each day by reflecting on all the things that went well, or you could look for things that make you smile as you go about your day (such as an unexpected hug or bumping into an old friend). Some people find it useful to have a dedicated gratitude journal in which they write down three things they are grateful for every morning or evening. By training your mind to notice what's right in life rather than what's wrong, you'll have more emotional strength reserves to tap into to help you bounce back from the stresses and strains of life.

Happiness is a way of travel, not a destination.

Roy M. Goodman

EXTRAORDINARY LIVES

The bigger your dreams and goals, the more likely it is that you will face hurdles along the way. When this happens, will you give up or persevere? A simple way to strengthen your inner resolve is to read about other people who have overcome great odds. From famous figures such as Winston Churchill and Rosa Parks to lesser-known heroes throughout the arts and sciences, seek out true-life stories of courage and resilience and draw strength from their examples.

Ever **tried**. Ever failed.
No matter. Try again.
Fail again. Fail **better**.

Samuel Beckett

Mastering others is strength. Mastering yourself is true power.

Lao Tzu

LEARN TO BREATHE

'Learning to breathe' sounds like a strange thing. After all, we breathe all the time without thinking about it. However, many of us take short, shallow breaths and, as a result, are depriving our bodies of much-needed oxygen. Breathing deeply nourishes our systems. It increases our energy and mental clarity, and it switches on the parasympathetic nervous system, which calms us. The next time you encounter a stressful situation or realise you are feeling anxious, place your hand on your stomach and take a deep breath into your navel, letting your body relax and fill with air. Then exhale s-l-o-w-l-y. Repeat five times or until you feel calm. Several times throughout the day, tune in to your breathing. Is your stomach clenched? Are you taking shallow breaths from your chest? Are you holding your breath? If so, practise a few rounds of deep breathing. If done regularly, this will gently retrain your body to breathe correctly.

THERE ARE TWO WAYS OF MEETING DIFFICULTIES: YOU ALTER THE DIFFICULTIES OR YOU ALTER YOURSELF MEETING THEM.

Phyllis Bottome

All of us suffer
difficulties in our lives.
And if you say to
yourself 'find a way',
you'll make it through.

Diana Nyad

THE MAGIC OF SOLITUDE

There is so much pressure to be active and busy that it can be hard to justify spending time alone 'doing nothing'. However, periods of solitude can play a crucial part in building your emotional resilience. Time alone gives you a chance to stop and reflect. It allows you to tune in to who you are and what matters most to you. It encourages self-reliance and a feeling of being in the driving seat, rather than your life being controlled by external demands. Try taking regular time out for solitude, even if it's only 5 minutes a day to begin with. Meditate for a few minutes in the morning, eat your lunch in the park, listen to soothing music, or sit by a fire and gaze into the flames. Make a point of setting aside time for rest and reflection and see how much better you feel.

The world breaks
everyone, and afterward,
some are strong at
the broken places.

Ernest Hemingway

BE PART OF SOMETHING BIGGER

Spiritual beliefs can be a source of great strength in life. Whether you are religious or not, strengthening your connection to something bigger – such as God, nature or the universe – can both comfort and inspire you during dark times. Make time for contemplative practices such as prayer, meditation or spending time in nature. Studies show that people who are spiritual tend to be more emotionally resilient.

CHANGE YOUR ABC

Many of us believe that negative events cause us to behave in a certain way, but research reveals that our reactions are based on our individual thoughts about adversity. This explains why people respond differently to the same stressful situation. A person might experience adversity (A) in the form of their partner leaving them. They might then have the belief (B) that they are worthless. As a consequence (C), they would sink into despair and find it hard to summon the motivation to go out and meet new people. But another person in the same situation might recognise that their relationship hadn't been working for quite some time and that they are now free to meet someone who is right for them. They would feel sad about their relationship ending, but they would be optimistic about their future and decide to join some local clubs to widen their social circle. Reflecting carefully on the ABCs in your life will help you overcome difficulties rather than letting them overwhelm you.

With ordinary talent and **extraordinary** perseverance, all things are **attainable**.

Thomas Foxwell Buxton

It's the size of your
hope that's going to
determine how far
you'll go in your life.

John Johnson

YOGIC LIFE

The benefits of yoga go far beyond improving physical flexibility. Yoga can help you sleep better. It can stabilise your mood and reduce stress and anxiety. Challenging poses in particular can help you build confidence and inner strength, which can positively affect the rest of your life. There are lots of different styles of yoga, which means there's a class to suit everybody. Hatha yoga (a generic term for 'physical yoga practice') focuses on postures and breathing, including a short period of deep relaxation at the end of the class.

Vinyasa yoga focuses on a series of smoothly flowing movements which are synchronised with the breath. Iyenger yoga emphasises precise alignment and the use of props such as blocks, straps and belts. Kundalini yoga awakens energy in the spine through postures, meditation and mantras. And Ashtanga yoga is a strenuous series of flowing poses designed to build strength and endurance. Whichever style you choose, regular yoga practice can help you embrace the present moment and find a feeling of peace, even in difficult situations.

WE MUST ACCEPT FINITE DISAPPOINTMENT, BUT NEVER LOSE INFINITE HOPE.

Martin Luther King Jr

If we believe that
tomorrow will be
better, we can bear
a hardship today.

Thích Nhất Hạnh

AFFIRM YOUR STRENGTH

As the saying goes, 'What you think is what you become.' A powerful way to boost your confidence and fortitude is to repeat affirmations of strength to yourself. Experiment with different statements until you find one that resonates with you. For example, 'I am strong, whole and complete' or 'I can face any challenge'. Repeat your affirmation quietly or silently to yourself – at intervals throughout the day and whenever you face a setback or difficulty.

Hope is patience
with the lamp lit.

Tertullian

BABY STEPS

When faced with challenges in life, we can become paralysed with fear. Whether it's a big challenge, such as starting a new business, or a small challenge, such as starting a fitness regime, the key to success is to face the fear and take action. The easiest way to do this is to take a baby step. Pick one thing you're currently procrastinating about and think of at least five ways to take a step in the right direction. For example, if your goal is to get fit, you could begin with the baby step of doing one push-up or squat a day, or going for a 10-minute walk in your lunch break. Don't be put off by the size of the step. Small steps lead to big results over time. With each new step, your confidence and enthusiasm will grow. Keep moving towards your goal. Resilient people take action.

One may **walk** over
the highest mountain
one **step** at a time.

John Wanamaker

Difficulties are things
that show a person
what they are.

Epictetus

LET IT OUT

Honour your feelings and recognise that difficult emotions such as anger, depression and loneliness are a natural part of the human experience. Let your emotions out by having a good cry if you need to. Crying can help you to regain your emotional balance as it releases toxins that have built up in the body due to stress. You should find that you feel calmer and less anxious afterwards. Another good way to express your feelings is through a creative outlet such as painting, blogging or playing a musical instrument. Creative activities can reduce stress and help you to process your experiences and feelings. The options for self-expression are endless. Whether you write poems, take photographs or draw sketches, creative pursuits offer you the space to deal with a range of emotions in a healthy and constructive way. Find something that gives you release.

IF THERE IS A
SHIELD OF FAITH
THAT YOU CAN
KEEP UP AGAINST
DIFFICULTIES,
HUMOUR IS THE
TEFLON COATING.

Laurel Lea

When you make a
mistake, learn from
it, pick yourself up
and move on.

Dave Pelzer

VARIETY IS THE SPICE OF LIFE

If your days have a drudge-like quality to them, take a look at how much variety there is in your life. Participating in a range of activities keeps your body and mind stimulated and healthy. A multidimensional life will also protect you from being knocked off course by a single setback. When you're living a rounded life, a 'failure' in one area is less likely to demoralise you and make you feel like a failure overall.

Patience and perseverance have a magical effect before which difficulties disappear and obstacles vanish.

John Quincy Adams

LET GO OF THE LITTLE THINGS

Nothing will sap your strength more than dwelling on things that don't matter. Worrying about a friend who doesn't reply to a text message, or the driver who cuts you off on your way to work, is a waste of valuable time, energy and brainpower. Obsessing over trivial things won't accomplish anything other than making you feel tired and irritable. Save your energy for accomplishing what matters most – whether that's raising a loving family, running a successful business, or collecting money for a charitable cause. It will take conscious effort and practice, but you can train yourself to let go of the little things and focus your energy on the things you can control. Don't let negative energy weigh you down and prevent you from reaching your full potential.

If you would know
strength and
patience, welcome the
company of trees.

Hal Borland

We must free ourselves
of the hope that the
sea will ever rest.
We must learn to
sail in high winds.

Aristotle Onassis

CREATIVE SOLUTIONS

If your path is blocked, create an alternative route. Creativity is your ultimate weapon. For example, if you want to meditate but 'don't have time', practise mindfulness in the shower each morning. If you want to learn French but can't afford tuition, listen to an audio language lesson when you exercise. If you want to start saving but 'can't afford it', start putting £5 aside every month. Whenever you hit an obstacle, find a creative way to climb over it or go around it. Never let it stop you.

You can't turn back
the clock, but you can
wind it up again.

Bonnie Prudden

CULTIVATE COMPASSION

When faced with a setback, it's all too easy to be hard on ourselves – but that won't help a bit. If you have one cigarette after quitting, or fail to stick to a new study regime, beating yourself up is likely to start a downward spiral that can be hard to escape. Instead, practise self-compassion. You actually made an effort, which is more than some people ever achieve. Treat yourself with kindness, climb back in the saddle, and keep going.

Keep the faith, don't
lose your perseverance
and always trust
your gut instinct.

Paula Abdul

GOOD FOOD, GOOD MOOD

There is a strong connection between what you eat and how you feel. Eating a balanced diet will keep both your body and mind healthy. Aim to eat plenty of wholefoods such as fruit and vegetables, meat and fish, and nuts and seeds. Avoid highly processed, packaged food and fast food. While it's tempting to turn to sugary food and refined carbohydrates such as bagels and pasta when times are tough, this will only make you feel lethargic and less able to deal with stress. Instead, choose foods which soothe and calm, such as avocados, Greek yoghurt, salmon, eggs, asparagus, blueberries, spinach, nuts and camomile tea. Besides giving your body the nutrients it needs, making healthy dietary choices can help you feel positive and empowered.

WHEN THE WORLD SAYS, 'GIVE UP,' HOPE WHISPERS, 'TRY IT ONE MORE TIME.'

Anonymous

Stubbornly persist,
and you will find that
the limits of your
stubbornness go well
beyond the stubbornness
of your limits.

Robert Brault

I don't measure a
man's success by how
high he climbs but
how high he bounces
when he hits bottom.

George S. Patton

WHEN LIFE GIVES YOU LEMONS...

If you're stuck in a traffic jam on your way to work, how do you react? Do you accept the situation and take advantage of the extra time to listen to the radio, or do you tense up and sink into a bad mood? Whichever way you react, it won't change the situation. Resilient people make the most of whatever situation they find themselves in. In this way, a traffic jam becomes an opportunity rather than a waste of time.

Our greatest **glory**
is not in never falling,
but in **rising** every
time we fall.

Confucius

We don't even know
how strong we are
until we are forced
to bring that hidden
strength forward.

Isabel Allende

HAVE AN ARGUMENT WITH YOURSELF

Just because you believe something, doesn't make it true. Many beliefs which we have held for years – often since childhood – sabotage our resilience. Start challenging the beliefs which are holding you back. Psychologists recommend judging your beliefs on four criteria. Firstly, look at the evidence. Does it support or negate your belief? If your partner leaves you and you begin to question your worth, focus on the evidence that disputes this. Secondly, consider the alternatives. Rather than latching on to the bleakest explanation for a bad event, find a more positive explanation. Thirdly, what are the implications? When faced with a setback, try not to draw negative conclusions. And finally, think about usefulness. Question the utility of your beliefs – even the most negative situations can have hidden gifts in the end. So, whenever you recognise beliefs that are holding you back, try replacing them with new, more empowering ones.

If you fall behind, run faster. Never give up, never surrender, and rise up against the odds.

Jesse Jackson

LIGHTEN UP

Seeing the funny side of life can help you rise above painful situations. Don't assume a sense of humour is something you're born with, though. You can train your brain to see the lighter side. If you're struggling, take a step back in order to gain some perspective. Try not to take yourself too seriously. Note the absurd or ironic things that happen to you. A sense of humour won't cure all your problems, but it will make them a lot easier to deal with.

Perseverance is not
a long race; it is
many short races
one after the other.

Walter Elliot

WORDS OF INSPIRATION

Sometimes a comforting or positive word is all we need to motivate us to keep going. Consider keeping a book of inspirational quotes on your bedside table or in your bag, so you can dip into it on a regular basis. You could also write out your favourite uplifting quotes and put them in your wallet or on a bathroom mirror where you can see them every day.

LET PERSEVERANCE BE YOUR ENGINE AND HOPE YOUR FUEL.

H. Jackson Brown Jr

Success seems to
be largely a matter
of hanging on after
others have let go.

William Feather

LOOK AT THE BIGGER PICTURE

When you're going through a rough patch, try going outside at night and gazing up in awe at the stars. Reflect on the fact that you are a tiny speck on a beautiful planet in a universe of 100 thousand million stars (that's '1' with 29 zeros after it!). Viewing your life as part of a bigger picture can put your problems into perspective and help you face challenges with renewed strength.

Imaginary obstacles
are insurmountable.
Real ones aren't.

Barbara Sher

Act as if what
you do makes a
difference. It does.

William James

How wonderful it
is that nobody need
wait a single moment
before starting to
improve the world.

Anne Frank

RETHINK STRESS

Begin to see stress as a professional athlete views his or her workout – as an opportunity to grow stronger. Stress builds character. It tests your resolve and problem-solving abilities. Look at it as a workout for your mind. Or turn it into a game and challenge yourself: how calmly can you steer through life, despite the bumps in the road? Viewing stress in a more positive light can help you embrace life's challenges and obstacles.

Great works are performed not by strength but by perseverance.

Samuel Johnson

STOP THE WHAT IFS

When things go wrong it can be easy to let your thoughts run away with you. Constantly imagining the very worst possible scenario or outcome is something psychologists call 'catastrophising'. For example, let's say you haven't hit your monthly sales target at work. This sets off a chain reaction of negative thinking in which you see yourself losing your job, going bankrupt, and your marriage breaking up. As soon as you realise you are overreacting like this, take a step back from your thoughts. Challenge how logical they are. It might help to put your thoughts onto paper. Does not hitting your sales target for one month really mean you will lose your job, marriage and financial security? Or is the reality that you have performed well in the past and there are things you can do next month to improve your sales? Stopping yourself from catastrophising takes a lot of conscious effort, but if you continually challenge your irrational thoughts, you will feel less demoralised and you will be motivated to take action to make things better.

THE CAVE
YOU FEAR TO
ENTER HOLDS
THE TREASURE
YOU SEEK.

Joseph Campbell

Whether you think
you can, or think you
can't, you are right.

Henry Ford

LESSONS IN FAILURE

No one is immune to failure. We all experience disappointments, frustrations and bruised egos from time to time. However, resilient people don't let failure stop them. They find the lessons hidden within these difficult moments and use these to help them overcome their next challenge. If you've made a mistake or something's gone disastrously wrong, take a little bit of time to reflect. Ask yourself some constructive questions. What did I do right? What could I have done better? What's the lesson here? Entrepreneurs, scientists, inventors and leaders all know there can be no success without failure. Most people experience catastrophes in some form or other, including financial problems, breakdowns and relationships ending. Successful souls manage to pick themselves up and persevere, armed with greater knowledge and wisdom.

What lies **behind** us and what lies before us are **tiny** matters compared to what lies **within** us.

Ralph Waldo Emerson

In the middle
of difficulty lies
opportunity.

Albert Einstein

RATION YOUR WILLPOWER

Resilient people may seem to have superhuman willpower, but the truth is that they have learnt to use their willpower wisely. Research shows we each have a finite amount of willpower and it fades throughout the day. Each decision and act of self-control we make depletes willpower from our inner reserves. So if you spend the day juggling stressful tasks and suppressing the urge to shout at a colleague, it's no wonder you come home in the evening and give in to your sugar cravings. The first step to maximising your willpower is to look after yourself. Exercising regularly, eating healthily, and getting a good night's sleep will help to top up your energy levels. If you're hungry and tired, your self-discipline is more likely to falter. In addition to this, try not to take on too many things at once. Avoid being in a position where you need lots of drive and determination every day. Spread demanding tasks over several days and mix them up with less demanding ones. Using your willpower wisely will help to recharge your inner strength.

BELIEVE IT!

When you adopt a new, empowering belief with absolute certainty, you can accomplish virtually anything. Here are five inspiring beliefs to try out:

- There is always a way if I'm committed.
- The past does not equal the future.
- There are no failures – only outcomes I can learn from.
- Everything happens for a reason.
- I create my own life.

Never give up, for that
is just the place and time
that the tide will turn.

Harriet Beecher Stowe

EXPECT GOOD THINGS

Our brains are wired to find the things we're looking for – so if you're always focusing on the negative and waiting for things to go wrong, your life will reflect that. The quickest way to recover from a setback is to tell yourself that things will get better. An optimistic outlook will lift your mood. It will motivate you to take action and persevere, which will drastically increase your chances of success. As Winston Churchill famously said, 'I'm an optimist. It does not seem too much use being anything else.' From now on, focus on things going right. Try visualising what you want, rather than worrying about what you fear. Envisaging the light at the end of the tunnel can fuel you with the strength to get through a tough patch.

ONCE YOU CHOOSE HOPE, ANYTHING'S POSSIBLE.

Christopher Reeve

The choice to have
a great attitude is
something that nobody
or no circumstance
can take from you.

Zig Ziglar

WARRIOR BODY

It's easier to face adversity when you're feeling fit and strong. Take care of yourself by exercising regularly. Experts recommend around 30 minutes of physical activity each day. Exercise helps build resilience in several ways: it produces endorphins and serotonin which lift your spirits, and it changes the way your brain responds to stress, making it more resistant to anxiety. It can also increase your energy, boost your confidence, and promote better sleep, all of which will help you to bounce back from stressful situations. The best way to start a fitness regime is to experiment with different exercises and activities until you find something you really enjoy. Any activity counts if it raises your heart rate and makes you breathe faster and feel warmer, whether it's brisk walking, dancing, rollerblading or swimming. Signing up for a team sport or exercise class, or exercising with a friend, can motivate you to stick with it and work harder. It also makes getting fit more fun!

If we are facing in the **right** direction, all we have to do is keep on **walking**.

Buddhist proverb

Difficulties strengthen
the mind, as labour
does the body.

Seneca the Younger

GO ON A MIND VACATION

Giving yourself a break from your busy mind can be restorative and healing. Mindful meditation is a practice which involves paying attention to the present moment and being aware of thoughts, accepting them without judgement. This helps us break out of habitual and often negative patterns of thinking. You can learn mindfulness from books, CDs, online tutorials or classes. A simple way to get started is to sit quietly for a few minutes and close your eyes. Bring your awareness to your breathing. Focus on the rise and fall of your chest or stomach, or on the sensation of air going in and out of your nostrils. If your attention wavers and you realise you are lost in your thoughts, gently bring your attention back to the physical sensations of breathing. Avoid the tendency to label your thoughts and feelings as good or bad – simply let them go and return to your breathing. After a few minutes, gently open your eyes and notice how you are feeling. Scientists say mindfulness can help us tolerate stress and deal with challenges more calmly and effectively.

DON'T BE DISCOURAGED. IT'S OFTEN THE LAST KEY IN THE BUNCH THAT OPENS THE LOCK.

Anonymous

A little more persistence,
a little more effort, and
what seemed hopeless
failure may turn to
glorious success.

Elbert Hubbard

DEAR DIARY

If your mind is swirling, spending some time putting your thoughts onto paper can help. People who regularly write in a diary or journal say that it calms them and helps them to emotionally process their day. Expressive writing is also a great way to clear your mind and work through solutions your to problems. If you would like to try this, find a quiet time and place and write continuously for 15–20 minutes. Write quickly and try not to judge or censor your writing. You can write about your feelings, create a poem, or even jot down song lyrics to express your emotions. Your journaling will be most effective if you do it on a regular basis. Many people say that their diary quickly becomes a trusted friend.

When we long for life
without difficulties,
remind us that oaks
grow strong in contrary
winds and diamonds are
made under pressure.

Peter Marshall

REDIRECT YOUR MIND

Ruminating on worries and problems can trigger a downward spiral. If you find yourself replaying upsetting events in your mind or imagining horrible scenarios, try distracting yourself. Be careful which distraction you choose, though. Many people try to numb unpleasant thoughts and feelings by watching television, drinking alcohol or comfort-eating. Healthier, more uplifting distractions include going to the gym, seeing a movie with friends, reading a positive book, heading out for a walk, or doing some baking.

NATURE'S MEDICINE

Make walking and being outside in nature a regular part of your routine. The fresh air, exercise and contact with nature are guaranteed to raise your spirits. Studies show just 5 minutes in a green space can reduce blood pressure, and a 20- to 30-minute walk can have the same calming effect as a mild tranquiliser. A walk can also be a good way to get a fresh perspective on things if you're feeling troubled, especially if it's a sunny day, as sunlight triggers the body to produce mood-boosting vitamin D. Besides walking, there are lots of other ways to connect with nature – you could spend more time in your garden, get an allotment and grow your own food, or volunteer with a local conservation group. Research shows that taking part in these activities can improve your mood, ease muscle tension, and positively affect your mental well-being.

You have **power** over your mind – not outside events. Realise this, and you will find **strength**.

Marcus Aurelius

The turning point
in the process of
growing up is when
you discover the core
of strength within you
that survives all hurt.

Max Lerner

BUILD YOUR COPING RESOURCES

Mentally strong people recognise they won't be able to combat stress if they're worn out and running on empty. They take regular time out to relax and recharge their batteries. Consider taking up meditation, yoga, t'ai chi or some other relaxation technique. These activities will help you unwind after a stressful day and help you remain calm during times of stress in the future. Make time to pamper yourself, too – whether that involves curling up on the sofa with a good book or getting a regular massage. Taking time out isn't self-indulgent; it's an essential strategy for coping with the ups and downs of life. Problems are easier to overcome from a state of relaxation. When we release the tension in our bodies and calm our minds, our creativity and problem-solving skills can come to the fore.

THAT'S ONE THING YOU LEARN IN SPORTS. YOU DON'T GIVE UP; YOU FIGHT TO THE FINISH.

Louis Zamperini

It's not that I'm so smart, it's just that I stay with problems longer.

Albert Einstein

TELL A DIFFERENT STORY

While we can't control exactly what happens in life, we can control what we tell ourselves about what's happened. Emotionally robust people have the ability to reframe situations, even when they seem challenging or scary. By looking for value and meaning in stressful events they are able to see 'bad' experiences in a positive light. For example, instead of seeing obstacles as stopping you from achieving your goals, you see them as opportunities to adapt and grow. Instead of fearing failure, you see failure as a necessary stepping stone on the way to success. Reframing is a powerful way to transform your thinking and boost your mental toughness. It won't change the situation, but it will put things into a healthier perspective and keep you motivated to keep going. Try it and see what a big difference it makes.

We don't develop courage by being happy every day. We develop it by surviving difficult times and challenging adversity.

Barbara De Angelis

IT'S YOUR CHOICE

Mentally strong people take responsibility for their life. They don't blame other people for 'making them feel bad' or 'messing up their day'. Instead, they take control of their own thoughts, feelings and behaviour. They understand that life isn't always easy or fair, but they don't sit around feeling sorry for themselves. Resilient people acknowledge that everything they do, from the time they wake up until the time they go to sleep at night, is a choice.

FUN MATTERS

Fun activities are great stress relievers. They give us a zest for life. However, with the responsibilities of adult life, many of us have lost our sense of playfulness. To introduce more fun into your life, start by writing down what you love doing – going for a bike ride, cuddling your kids, pottering in the garden or learning how to juggle, for example. Next, take a long, hard look at the past week and note how much time you put aside for these things. The irony is that when we're under pressure we often stop doing the very things that boost our mood and build our resilience. From now on, schedule regular time in your diary to have fun. A great way to recapture your sense of joy is to try something you once loved doing as a kid – you could throw a Frisbee, play a board game, fly a kite or learn a magic trick.

Fall seven times,
stand up eight.

Japanese proverb

It's not the winning that teaches you how to be resilient. It's the setback. It's the loss.

Beth Brooke

GET COMFORTABLE WITH BEING UNCOMFORTABLE

Life isn't easy. We may struggle when we have to move home or experience the loss of a friendship. Strong people accept that change is part of life. They understand that in order for things to improve, they may need to go through some discomfort and uncertainty – whether that's going to job interviews or meeting a financial advisor to sort out their money troubles. You can build up your resilience by stepping outside of your comfort zone more frequently. Start by trying new things

– new foods, new routes to work and so on. If you're feeling more adventurous, you could volunteer in your community, take singing lessons, or learn a new language. Every time you step outside of your comfort zone, you'll increase your tolerance for uncertainty. It may be hard at first but the rewards in the end will be worth it. With uncertainty come new experiences and new opportunities.

WHEN YOU COME TO THE END OF YOUR ROPE, TIE A KNOT AND HANG ON.

Anonymous

Everyone goes through adversity in life, but what matters is how you learn from it.

Lou Holtz

STRUGGLES LEAD TO STRENGTH

The strongest tree in the forest is not the one that is protected from the wind and rain. The strongest trees are the ones that are exposed to the elements. They develop deep roots and stout trunks in order to survive. In the same way, the struggles we face and overcome in life make us stronger. Reminding yourself of this fact can help you weather the storms of life.

You don't learn to walk
by following the rules.
You learn by doing,
and by falling over.

Richard Branson

PEOPLE POWER

It's important to spend time with people who nurture and support you, especially during times of crisis. Being around positive people can uplift you and help you feel less isolated. Friends and family can also act as sounding boards, offering feedback and advice and helping you gain a sense of perspective. If keeping in touch with your friends has dwindled to the odd email, text or Facebook post, pick up the phone or arrange to meet for a coffee. Face-to-face interaction helps build trust and brings with it the possibility of hugs and laughter. Laughter triggers the release of endorphins, the body's happy chemicals, and a hug triggers the release of oxytocin, which lowers our blood pressure and reduces stress and anxiety. Build a community of positive people around you and reach out for help whenever you need support.

See any **detour** as
an opportunity to
experience **new** things.

H. Jackson Brown Jr

It takes no more time
to see the good side of
life than to see the bad.

Jimmy Buffett

FACE REALITY

No one is immune to setbacks. They happen to everyone. The question is, when misfortune occurs, do you waste time and energy resisting what is happening or do you put all your energy into doing what you can to move forward? If you find yourself regularly thinking things like, 'I shouldn't have to deal with this' and 'Why me?' you may be fighting reality. Resilient people accept the reality they are faced with, even if it's uncomfortable, and focus all their energy on changing the circumstance or improving their coping abilities.

There are plenty of
difficult obstacles
in your path. Don't
allow yourself to
become one of them.

Ralph Marston

KEEP CALM AND CARRY ON

One of the most important keys to resilience during tough times is to control your emotions. It's very easy to get swept away by what is happening and slip into negative thinking. Resilient people are able to remain calm and focused, despite the turmoil that may be surrounding them. One of the best ways to build this skill is to practise remaining calm and focused in everyday situations. If you practise on the little things, calmness will become a habit that will kick in when you need it most. The next time you're stuck in a traffic jam or your bag breaks and empties your shopping all over the floor, try remaining cool and calm. The regular practice of yoga, meditation or mindfulness can also help you with this.

MAN NEVER MADE ANY MATERIAL AS RESILIENT AS THE HUMAN SPIRIT.

Bernard Williams

Never, never,
never give up.

Winston Churchill

TIME FOR BED

Sleep keeps us both mentally and physically strong. Just one night of bad sleep can cause us to feel negative, irritable and more easily overwhelmed the next day. Most adults need at least 7–8 hours' sleep a night but everyone is different. If you wake up feeling refreshed, you're probably getting enough sleep. If you're not getting enough sleep, the following tips will help: take time to unwind before bed – dim the lights, listen to calming music, have a bath, or meditate. Turn your bedroom into a relaxing space by removing any clutter and painting the walls a neutral, calming colour. Ensure your bedroom is as dark as possible – ban electronic gadgets and consider getting thicker curtains or blackout blinds. If your mind is racing, try jotting down your thoughts in a diary. These simple actions can turn your bedroom into a peaceful sanctuary and encourage a better night's sleep.

the little book of
POSITIVITY

lucy lane

THE LITTLE BOOK OF POSITIVITY

Lucy Lane

£5.99
Hardback
ISBN: 978-1-84953-788-9

In a world where we're constantly bombarded by work and worry, we all need a little boost to our happiness levels now and then. This book of inspiring quotations and simple, easy-to-follow tips provides you with practical advice on thinking positively and achieving a more balanced attitude to life.

the little book of
RELAXATION

lucy lane

THE LITTLE BOOK OF RELAXATION

Lucy Lane

£5.99
Hardback
ISBN: 978-1-84953-787-2

This essential pocket-sized companion is packed with inspiring quotations from writers, spiritual leaders and philosophers, along with simple but effective tips to help you bring moments of calm into your daily life. *The Little Book of Relaxation* will benefit the mind and heart and make a real difference to every day.

If you're interested in finding out
more about our books, find us on
Facebook at **Summersdale Publishers**
and follow us on Twitter
at **@Summersdale.**

www.summersdale.com